The Brontës

David Orme

Published by Evans Brothers Limited
2A Portman Mansions
Chiltern Street
London W1M 1LE

© Evans Brothers Limited 1999

First published 1999

Printed at Oriental Press, Dubai, U.A.E.

ISBN 0 237 51744 2

British Cataloguing in Publication Data

Orme, David
    The Brontës. - (Writers in Britain)
    1. Brontë, Anne, 1820-1849 - Criticism and interpretation - Juvenile literature 2. Brontë, Branwell, 1817-1848 - Criticism and interpretation - Juvenile literature 3. Brontë, Charlotte, 1816-1855 - Criticism and interpretation - Juvenile literature 4. Brontë, Emily, 1818-1848 - Criticism and interpretation - Juvenile literature 5. Great Britain - Social conditions - 19th century - Juvenile literature
    1. Title
    823.8'09

This book is dedicated to Eileen Bird

Acknowledgements

Consultant – Sharon Courtney, Education Officer, the Brontë Society

Editor – Su Swallow
Designer – Ann Samuel
Production – Jenny Mulvanny
Picture Research – Victoria Brooker

For permission to reproduce copyright material, the author and publishers gratefully acknowledge the following:

cover (left) National Portrait Gallery/Bridgeman Art Library (top right) Robert Harding Picture Library (bottom right) Aquarius Picture Library **title page** Illustration by E.H.Shepard reproduced by permission of Curtis Brown Ltd, London, on behalf of the artist's estate. Chris Beetles Ltd./Bridgeman Art Library **page 5** Mary Evans Picture Library **page 6** Museum of British Transport/Bridgeman Art Library **page 7** (top) Private Collection/Bridgeman Art Library (bottom) © The Brontë Society **page 8** (top) Hulton Getty (bottom) Robert Harding Picture Library **page 9** (top left) National Portrait Gallery/Bridgeman Art Library (top right) Hulton Getty (bottom) © The Brontë Society **page 10** (top and bottom) © The Brontë Society **page 11** (top) Private Collection/Bridgeman Art Library (bottom) Hulton Getty **page 12** (top) Apsley House, The Wellington Museum/Bridgeman Art Library (bottom) V&A Picture Library **page 13** © The Brontë Society **page 14** Aquarius Picture Library **page 15** (top) Hulton Getty (middle) © The Brontë Society (bottom) Christie's Images/Bridgeman Art Library **page 16** (top) Mary Evans Picture Library (bottom) Private Collection/Bridgeman Art Library **page 17** (top) Max Payne (bottom) Hulton Getty **page 18** Aquarius Library **page 19** (top) Aquarius Library (bottom) National Portrait Gallery/Bridgeman Art Library **page 20** (top) Hulton Getty (bottom) Aquarius Library **page 21** (top) The Ronald Grant Archive (bottom) Mary Evans Picture Library **page 22** Aquarius Library **page 23** (top) Aquarius Library (bottom) Mary Evans Picture Library **page 24** Hulton Getty **page 25** (top) © The Brontë Society (bottom) Hulton Getty **page 26** (top) National Portrait Gallery/Bridgeman Art Library (bottom) Aquarius Library **page 27** (top) Aquarius Library (bottom) Illustration by E.H.Shepard reproduced by permission of Curtis Brown Ltd, London, on behalf of the artist's estate.Chris Beetles Ltd./Bridgeman Art Library

Contents

Time of change 1815-1850

Travel and communication

The Reverend Patrick Brontë married Maria Branwell in 1812. In 1820 their last and sixth child, Anne, was born. By 1855, when Charlotte Brontë died, Patrick had lost all his children.

The Brontë children lived short lives – none of them lived to reach 40 – yet they would have witnessed enormous changes. As children, any journey would have been a long and arduous affair. Only the well-to-do could afford to travel by carriage – walking was the only option for the poor. Long journeys could take many days. By 1842 the 26-year-old Charlotte was able to travel by train from Leeds to London in 11 hours.

In 1840, the universal penny post was introduced. Victorians were great letter writers, the Brontës included, and this innovation enabled them to write not just to their local friends and acquaintances but also to the great literary figures of the day. Other developments, such as the telegraph and the growth of newspapers, meant that even remote backwaters such as Haworth were now in touch with national and world events.

1830–1850 was a time of great railway construction. By the end of this period all the great cities of Britain were linked.

66 *Suddenly there was a general feeling in the country that the whole surface of the land should be transformed and covered, as by a network, with these mighty means of communication. The immediate effect on the condition of the country was absolutely prodigious.* 99

Benjamin Disraeli

Revolution and Reform

During the lifetime of the Brontës the Industrial Revolution was at its height. The only significant industry of the West Riding of Yorkshire, where they lived, was the production of wool. Traditionally, weaving was done by individual weavers working in cottages near the source of the wool supply. By the early nineteenth century, mechanical looms had been developed, resulting in the growth of huge mills. At first, these were powered by water and needed to be sited by large rivers. Hand-loom weavers could no longer compete. This led to riots, machine-smashing and murder. Inevitably, the mill-owners triumphed, creating on the one hand a wealthy new class of self-made men, and on the other hand widespread rural poverty. Charlotte described these events in her novel *Shirley*; she may have heard accounts of the Luddites (people who fought against the changes) from her father. The second decade of the nineteenth century was a time of depression and destitution, and the rise of radical ideas. Protest culminated in the 'Peterloo' massacre in 1819. The radical thinker Henry Hunt attempted to address a crowd of over 60,000 in Manchester; Hunt was arrested and soldiers turned on the crowd. However, the seeds of reform had taken root and by 1832 the great Reform Bill had started the process that would lead ultimately to universal suffrage and modern democracy.

One of the great mills that brought industry to rural Yorkshire.

The Brontës' attempt to start a school of their own, 1841

The Misses Bronte's Establishment

FOR

THE BOARD AND EDUCATION

OF A LIMITED NUMBER OF

YOUNG LADIES,

THE PARSONAGE, HAWORTH,

NEAR BRADFORD.

Terms.

	£.	s.	d.
BOARD AND EDUCATION, including Writing, Arithmetic, History, Grammar, Geography, and Needle Work, per Annum,	35	0	0
French, German, Latin — each per Quarter,	1	1	0
Music, Drawing, — each per Quarter,	1	1	0
Use of Piano Forte, per Quarter,	0	5	0
Washing, per Quarter,	0	15	0

Each Young Lady to be provided with One Pair of Sheets, Pillow Cases, Four Towels, a Dessert and Tea-spoon.

A Quarter's Notice, or a Quarter's Board, is required previous to the Removal of a Pupil.

Education

These years saw an enormous growth in the demand for education. For the first time, education for girls beyond mere domestic skills was seen as important. The schools attended by the Brontë girls had sprung up to answer this need. Teaching in such schools became a new career option for women – both Charlotte and Emily became teachers for a while. They even drew up plans to open a school of their own, although this never happened.

The Brontë family

Patrick Brontë in later life

Patrick and Maria

Life was not easy for Patrick Brontë and his wife Maria. His only income was his earnings as a clergyman, and he was hard pressed to support his growing family. By 1820 the Brontës had six children, and the vicarage at Thornton, where they lived, was bursting at the seams. In that year Patrick became curate of Haworth, where he remained for the rest of his life. He outlived the rest of his family, dying in 1861.

Both Patrick and Maria were active writers. Patrick published two books of poems. Some of his poems show his great love of nature in all its moods, which he passed on to his children. Seeing their father's work in print was an enormous encouragement to the young Brontës from an early age. The Brontë parents were also great letter writers, a habit which their children inherited.

In 1821, Maria died of cancer, leaving Patrick to bring up his six children alone. His search for another wife was not successful and eventually the children's aunt, Maria's sister Elizabeth, came to Yorkshire to look after them.

Haworth Parsonage as it is today. It is the home of the Brontë museum.

The Brontë children

Patrick and Maria's first child was a girl, Maria, born in 1814. She was followed by Elizabeth, in 1815, Charlotte in 1816, Patrick Branwell, their only son, in 1817, Emily in 1818 and Anne in 1820. Maria and Elizabeth died of tuberculosis in 1825.

Charlotte, Emily and Anne all became published writers. To begin with, they wrote under pseudonyms (pen-names) suggesting that they were male rather than female – Currer, Ellis, and Acton Bell. Their first book was a collection of poems, published in 1846. In 1847 *Jane Eyre* by Charlotte (Currer Bell), *Wuthering Heights* by Emily (Ellis Bell) and *Agnes Grey* by Anne (Acton Bell) were published. Emily died in 1848. In that year Anne published *The Tenant of Wildfell Hall* – but by 1849 she too was

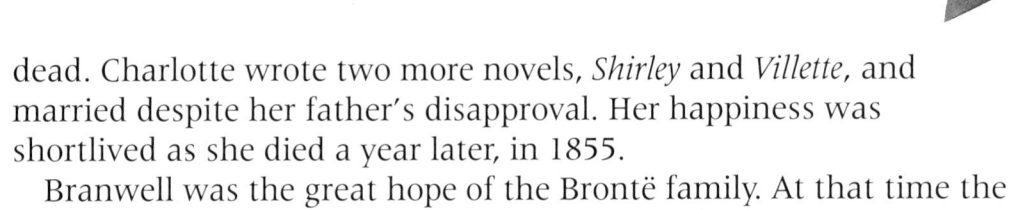

Charlotte, Emily and Anne, painted by their brother Branwell

Branwell had some talent as a writer, and he was encouraged by Hartley Coleridge, one of the leading writers of the day, to devote his life to it.

dead. Charlotte wrote two more novels, *Shirley* and *Villette*, and married despite her father's disapproval. Her happiness was shortlived as she died a year later, in 1855.

Branwell was the great hope of the Brontë family. At that time the role of women was to look after the house and family – careers were for men only. Unfortunately, Branwell Brontë did not live up to his father's expectations. To begin with, he too wanted to be a writer. Some of his poems were published in local newspapers and he

started a novel of his own. He showed some talent as a portrait painter, but he did not have the dedication to become successful. He became a private tutor, and then a railway clerk. Even in this work he was not successful, and after 18 months he was given the sack.

Increasingly Branwell became a disappointment to the family. He was frequently drunk, and almost certainly took opium. By 1848, he too had died.

Branwell's sisters were talented artists. Emily drew this picture of Anne's spaniel, Flossy.

Life at Haworth – and beyond

The dining room at Haworth Parsonage, looking as it did at the time of the Brontës

Life at the Parsonage

Despite many tragedies, the Brontë sisters, and their brother Branwell, had a happy home at Haworth. Their father Patrick has been described as an eccentric, even cruel man, and his upbringing of his children harsh and rigid. The Parsonage was described not long after Charlotte's death as 'grim, solitary, neglected, and wretched looking.' However, most of the stories about the unhappy childhood of the Brontës are exaggerated, or simply not true.

It seems that their aunt Elizabeth, who came to look after them after the death of their mother, was not particularly affectionate, but the children enjoyed their own company, and that of the long-time family servant Tabitha Aykroyd. In the mornings the girls took lessons with their aunt – the emphasis was on domestic matters such as needlework – while Branwell learnt Latin and Greek with his father. In the afternoons they were free to roam the moors. The Brontës were great animal lovers, and the Parsonage was full of dogs, cats, and injured wild animals brought in to be cared for.

Storytelling was an important part of their lives. Their father would tell them tales over the breakfast table, full of quiet humour. Candles were expensive, so during long winter evenings they would sit by the fire and tell stories from imagination, or listen while Tabitha told them strange and supernatural folk tales of Yorkshire.

Top Withens, Haworth Moor – the possible inspiration for *Wuthering Heights*

Mass education

During most of the nineteenth century, education was only available for those who could afford it. By the 1830s churches and charities were beginning to set up schools for poorer children, using the monitor system – the teacher taught the older children, who in turn taught the younger ones.

In 1833 the government provided the first public money for school building, but elementary schooling was not made compulsory for all children until 1880.

School life – pupils and teachers

In 1824 the girls were sent to the School for the Daughters of Clergymen at Cowan Bridge. Conditions were very bad, and Charlotte used the experience there when she described Lowood in *Jane Eyre*. The portrait of the Reverend Mr Brocklehurst in *Jane Eyre* was based on the owner of Cowan Bridge, the Reverend Carus Wilson, a severe and gloomy-minded disciplinarian.

The Clergy Daughters' School at Cowan Bridge as it looks today

> *...whenever the famished great girls had an opportunity, they would coax or menace the little ones out of their portion. Many a time I have shared between two claimants the precious morsel of brown bread distributed at teatime; and after relinquishing to a third half the contents of my mug of coffee, I have swallowed the remainder with an accompaniment of secret tears, forced from me by the exigency of hunger.*
>
> From *Jane Eyre*

During the 1830s the three Brontë girls went to Roe Head School. Conditions here were certainly an improvement and Charlotte in particular met life-long friends. In 1835 Charlotte worked at the school as a teacher. The duties were hard and not all her pupils were very bright. However, the Brontë girls knew that they would have to earn a living, and opportunities were limited. Each of the girls took jobs as governesses.

A scene at Lowood from the 1943 film of *Jane Eyre*

> *Reads little - Writes indifferently - ciphers a little and works neatly. Knows nothing of Grammar, Geography, or Accomplishments. Although clever of her age knows nothing systematically.*
>
> Charlotte Brontë's school report, aged 8

Most well-off families would employ a governess to take charge of children and provide them with an education. For many poor but intelligent women of a certain class, it was the only profession open to them. Like teaching, the hours were long and the pay poor. Having difficult and unruly children to deal with made it far worse. In her first job as a governess, Anne Brontë is said to have tied two of the children to a table leg to make them do their lessons – not surprisingly, she was dismissed!

The Brontës as writers and readers

Reading

Reading matter for the young Brontës was limited; there were few children's books published at that time. Patrick Brontë had books of his own, and nearby Keighley had a small subscription library which they no doubt made use of as they grew older.

Local newspapers such as the *Leeds Intelligencer*, the *Leeds Mercury* and the *Halifax Guardian*, and magazines such as Blackwood's, were important to the Brontës. Local newspapers did the job of national newspapers today, and carried foreign news and news of national politics. The letter columns of local papers were full of lively debate on issues of the time. The Brontës read as widely as they could; they especially enjoyed the novels of Walter Scott. They followed news of national and international events closely, particularly news of their great hero Arthur Wellesley, the Duke of Wellington.

Arthur Wellesley, 1st Duke of Wellington, soldier and statesman who routed Napoleon at Waterloo in 1815 and became Prime Minister in 1828.

Glasstown and Gondal

The humdrum lives of the Brontës left them plenty of time to exercise their imaginations, through storytelling and play. Inevitably, this was to lead to the first attempts at writing.

In June of 1826 Patrick Brontë brought home presents for his children: a doll for Anne, ninepins for Charlotte, a toy village for Emily, and a set of 12 toy soldiers for Branwell. The toy soldiers excited all of the children. Charlotte writes:

'Emily and me jumped out of bed and I snatched up one and exclaimed this is the Duke of Wellington, it shall be mine… Emily likewise took one and said it should be hers.'

The soldiers were given names, and characters of their own. Soon these characters started to appear in games, and by 1829 in stories written by the children.

It was toy soldiers like these that inspired the early writing of the Brontë children.

More and more stories followed, describing the imaginary kingdom of Glasstown somewhere in Africa, which had the Duke of Wellington as king. The stories created a complete imaginary history of the kingdom, complete with battles, revolutions, and thrilling adventures.

The writing of these stories continued for over ten years, and eventually the amount of material produced was greater than all the published work of the Brontës put together.

> 66 *Rogue is about 47 years of age. His manner is rather polished and gentlemanly, but his mind is deceitful, bloody and cruel. His walk (in which he much prides himself) is stately and soldier-like, and he fancies that it greatly resembles that of the Duke of Wellington.* 99
>
> Description of a Glasstown pirate by Charlotte, 1829

Charlotte and Branwell were the leading players in the Glasstown stories. Around 1834 Emily and Anne created their own kingdom of Gondal. The writing was a mix of stories and poems.

The 'juvenile' writing of the Brontës continued into adulthood – Emily and Anne were still adding to the Gondal saga in 1845, when Anne was 25 and Emily 27. Only two years later *Jane Eyre*, *Wuthering Heights* and *Agnes Grey* were published.

Spelling

The Brontës were not particularly skilful in spelling and punctuation! This is an extract from Emily and Anne's Diary for November 24th, 1834. Emily was 16 and Anne 14.

It is past twelve o'clock Anne and I have not tided ourselvs, done our bed work or done our lessons and we want to go out to play We are going to have for Dinner Boiled Beef Turnips, potato's and applepudding the Kitchin in avery untidy state Anne and I have not Done our music excercise which consists of b majer Taby said on my putting a pen in her face Ya pitter pottering there instead of pilling a potatoe I answered O Dear, O Dear, O Dear, I will derictly with that I get up, take a Knife and begin pilling…

Some of the 'Little Books' written by the Brontë children

Women's role in society

Opportunities for women

At the beginning of the nineteenth century opportunities for women were very limited. Universities were closed to them, as were all of the major professions. Their role in life was regarded as almost entirely domestic – bringing up children, homemaking for their husbands. Women from well-to-do families were expected to be 'accomplished' in various ways – music, drawing, the writing of verse – but their work was unlikely to be taken seriously. On marrying, a woman's property, even her income from work, would belong to her husband.

Scene from a modern version of *Jane Eyre*

Working class women could obtain employment as servants; increasingly, there was work for women in the new industries such as the wool and cotton mills. For girls such as the Brontë sisters, daughters of a poor clergyman, the job of governess was one of a very limited number of options (see page 11).

Women as writers

> 66 *Literature cannot be the business of a woman's life, and it ought not to be. The more she is engaged in her proper duties, the less leisure she will have for it, even as an accomplishment and a recreation. To those duties you have not yet been called, and when you are you will be less eager for celebrity.* 99
>
> Letter from Robert Southey, Poet Laureate, to Charlotte Brontë, 1836

Despite Southey's views, there were a number of distinguished women writers to provide models and encouragement for the Brontës. Fanny Burney (1752–1840) was a distinguished woman of letters and the author of four successful novels. Ann Radcliffe (1764–1823) was popular for her 'gothic' tales full of supernatural happenings and thrilling events – *The Mysteries of Udolpho* (1794) is the best known.

The most distinguished of all novelists at the beginning of the nineteenth century was Jane Austen (1775–1817). Even she published her work anonymously to begin with – to seek to become a celebrity was considered improper and 'forward' for a woman.

Charlotte, Emily and Anne first wrote under the masculine-sounding pseudonyms of Currer, Ellis and Acton Bell. This caused some confusion among readers and reviewers. Some accepted the idea of three brothers; some thought that there was only one male author involved, using three different names.

The Brontë sisters as the Bell 'brothers'

> " *... we did not like to declare ourselves women because – without at that time suspecting that our mode of writing and thinking was not what is called 'feminine' – we had a vague impression that authoresses are likely to be looked on with prejudice.* "
> Charlotte Brontë

Although the Brontës were not feminists in the modern sense, they express the frustrations and limitations of their lives in their novels and letters. It may be that these frustrations came mainly from a shortage of money and the need to earn a living rather than a resentment at the way women were treated in society.

A page from Emily's diary, 26th June 1837

Charlotte was always the most willing to express a point of view through her writing. In *Jane Eyre*, she writes:

> " *Women are supposed to be very calm generally but women feel just as men feel; they need exercise for their faculties, and a field for their efforts as much as their brothers do; they suffer from too rigid a constraint, too absolute a stagnation, precisely as men would suffer.* "

A Victorian drawing room with women demonstrating their various accomplishments

Ever present death

$\mathcal{S}$udden death is a familiar event in the Brontë novels, particularly in *Wuthering Heights* – the reader begins to wonder if any of the characters will be left alive at the end of the novel! This may seem morbid and melodramatic to modern readers, but for Victorian families the premature death of friends and family members was something that had to be faced. By the time Emily published *Wuthering Heights* she had already lost her mother and her two eldest sisters, Elizabeth and Maria. The year following its publication she herself died. By the time Patrick Brontë died in 1861, his entire family was dead.

Haworth Church and Parsonage in 1857. All the Brontë children, except Anne, are buried here.

Haworth in the 1850s

Haworth Parsonage and graveyard as they look today

It might be imagined that Haworth, set in open countryside, would be a relatively healthy place at the time the Brontës lived there. This was certainly not so. The filthy conditions were breeding grounds for diseases such as typhoid, cholera and tuberculosis. The small houses were overcrowded, with some families living in damp cellars. The village had no sewers. Even the Brontë household had to make do with privies. All water had to be fetched from pumps. These were badly contaminated by human and animal sewage, and by bodies in the graveyard at the top of the hill.

Most people's diet was desperately poor; meals usually consisted of oatmeal, or potatoes. Inevitably the result was a high level of infant mortality. Over 40 per cent of children died before their sixth birthday; average life expectancy in Haworth was 25. Diet in the Brontë household was much better, and the parsonage had its own well of pure water. Even so, only four out of the six Brontë children lived to reach their thirties.

'Consumption'

In 1824 the four oldest of the Brontë sisters were sent away to school at Cowan Bridge. The conditions they found there were probably no worse than in any boarding school at the time, but they were not at all suitable to the little girls who had only just recovered from illness. The rooms were always cold and damp; the food largely inedible. It is not surprising that during the first winter there Maria and Elizabeth both developed tuberculosis, a disease then known as 'consumption'. Tuberculosis is an infection of the lungs, and is usually the result of poor living conditions. If it is not treated, patients waste away and eventually die. The two sisters died the following year.

Branwell Brontë died of tuberculosis, made worse by drink and drugs, in 1848. Emily Brontë caught cold at his funeral. It was soon discovered that she had the disease as well – it was not realised at the time that tuberculosis is very infectious. She died in December. Anne died the following May.

Anne Brontë's grave in Scarborough

Victorian sentimentality

The death of children frequently features in Victorian fiction. *Wuthering Heights* is sometimes criticised for 'making a meal' of the death of Linton. It needs to be remembered that sudden death, particularly of children, was commonplace: Emily had seen her elder sisters and her brother dying painfully. What is sentimental to the modern viewpoint was part of everyday life in early Victorian England.

> **On the death of Anne Brontë**
>
> 66 *There's little joy in life for me,*
> *And little terror in the grave;*
> *I've lived the parting hour to see*
> *Of one I would have died to save.* 99
>
> Charlotte Brontë, on the death of her sister Anne.

Cholera

Cholera was a major killer in the early nineteenth century. Until 1854 no-one knew that it was a water-borne disease. Up to that time it was assumed that the 'germs' of cholera came from bad air. Patients would have their windows left open even in winter in the hope of cure. The discovery of the true means of transmitting the disease came in London, when it was noticed that cholera victims drew their water from a particular pump; those who used a different pump were free of the disease. The handle was removed from the contaminated pump, and the outbreak was halted.

Fumigation with carbolic acid; one of the more ineffective ways to prevent cholera

Landscape and the weather

The Haworth Moors

The writing of the Brontës is heavily influenced by the landscape that surrounded them at Haworth and which is little changed today. The poor soils and unpredictable weather makes any agriculture other than traditional sheep-rearing very difficult.

The wild moorland was just a short walk from the parsonage, and the Brontë children roamed freely across it, revelling in the rugged beauty and the ever-changing weather. The landscape, untouched by industry or farming, represented a complete contrast to the life at the Parsonage, with its sense of order and routine. Here they could see demonstrated for them the Romantic idea that humankind represented order and reason, while the natural world, savage and unpredictable, was in conflict with it. Human beings were rational creatures, and yet inside them their dangerous 'animal' nature lurked In their explorations of the moors the Brontës were able to throw off the shackles of their restricted lives and taste freedom.

Inevitably the West Riding of Yorkshire, and in particular the moorland landscape, became the setting for the novels of the Brontës One reason for this was that it was the only place they knew – Charlotte did not see the sea until 1839 when she was 23.

Cathy in a stormy scene from a modern version of *Wuthering Heights*.

Landscape in *Wuthering Heights*

> 66 *Wuthering Heights is the name of Mr Heathcliff's dwelling, "wuthering" being a significant provincial adjective, descriptive of the atmospheric tumult to which its station is exposed in stormy weather.* 99
>
> *Wuthering Heights*, Chapter 1

The word 'wuthering' is full of suggestiveness – it seems to combine windiness, bleakness and sadness. All through the novel Emily Brontë uses the landscape and ever-changing weather to underline the events of the story. A sense of threatening menace is shown by the sultry build-up to a storm, as in Chapter 17 when Linton is discovered alone on the moor. At moments of great drama the rain

Charlotte wrote of Heathcliff, 'Tyranny and ignorance made of him a demon.'

When Emily wrote these lines of poetry she was working as a teacher at Law Hill School, near Halifax. The poem describes the 'green lane' that led from the Parsonage to the moors. Her feelings about her work at Law Hill and its 'dungeon bars' are made very clear.

> *A little and a lone green lane*
> *That opened on a common wide*
> *A distant, dreamy dim blue chain*
> *Of mountains circling every side –*
>
> *That was the scene – I knew it well*
> *I knew the path-ways far and near*
> *That winding o'er each billowy swell*
> *Marked out the tracks of wandering deer.*
>
> *Could I have lingered but an hour*
> *It well had paid a week of toil*
> *But truth has banished fancies power*
> *I hear my dungeon bars recoil.*
>
> Emily Brontë

and wind beat on the windows. The weather becomes a major character in the story. This strong visual quality has made the Brontë novel ideal for film-makers. The character of Heathcliff, too, seems to have been made from the landscape – he is wild, powerful, unpredictable, dangerous, and yet fascinating.

Emily does not write about the landscape with the eye of naturalist. *Wuthering Heights* is not full of details of the birds, plants and animals to be seen on the moors. Emily saw nature as a whole, as something almost alive in its changing moods. Some writers say her feelings about nature were almost religious, and that she felt that nature itself was in some way a living, supernatural force.

> ❝ *My sister Emily loved the moors. They were far more to her than a mere spectacle; they were what she lived in and by as much as the wild birds, their tenants, or the heather, their produce. She found in the bleak solitude many and dear delights; and not the least best loved was – liberty.* ❞
>
> Charlotte Brontë

A portrait of Emily by Branwell painted in about 1833

Dangerous heroes

Powerful characters

The description of the important male characters in the Brontë novels is one reason why the novels are still so widely read today. These characters, particularly Heathcliff in *Wuthering Heights* but also Rochester in *Jane Eyre* and Huntingdon in *The Tenant of Wildfell Hall*, are not simple or straightforward. It is this complexity of character that gives the novels of the Brontës their fascination.

Rochester

Rochester is a man with a 'hidden secret' – his arranged marriage to Bertha Mason, who is now mad. Charlotte Brontë describes him as a victim of circumstance; he is cruel, bullying and deceitful, but at the same time can show generosity, and recognises his own faults. 'I could reform – I have strength yet for that' says Rochester, 'but where is the use of thinking of it, hampered, burdened, cursed as I am? Besides, since happiness is irrevocably denied me, I have a right to get pleasure out of life: and I will get it, cost what it may.'

His desire to 'possess' Jane on his terms shows his selfishness, and yet he clearly loves her. At the end of the novel his attempts to save the life of the mad Bertha in the fire at Thornfield show him to be 'neither selfish nor self-indulgent' – a true hero.

In her description of Rochester's blindness Charlotte makes use of the experience of her father, who became blind with cataracts, and was nursed by Charlotte while she was writing *Jane Eyre*. Following a painful operation without anaesthetic Patrick Brontë, like Rochester, regained his sight.

Orson Wells as Rochester in the 1943 version of *Jane Eyre*

A modern Rochester

> 66 *Mr Rochester has a thoughtful nature and a very feeling heart: he is neither selfish nor self-indulgent: he is ill-educated, misguided; errs . . . through rashness and inexperience.*, 99
>
> Charlotte Brontë

Heathcliff

> *Nelly ... tell her what Heathcliff is: ...He's not a rough diamond – a pearl-containing oyster of a rustic: he's a fierce, pitiless, wolfish man. I know he couldn't love a Linton; and yet he'd be quite capable of marrying your fortune and expectations! Avarice is growing with him a besetting sin.*
>
> Catherine to Isabella, *Wuthering Heights*, Chapter 10

Throughout *Wuthering Heights* Heathcliff is described by one character after another as wicked, even evil. He is certainly cruel and vindictive, but, like Rochester, he is a victim of his own background and of his own nature. Heathcliff is a man of extremes, and even the positive side of his nature – his love for Catherine – is so obsessive as to lead to his own death. Some readers feel that despite all his faults, his greatness shines through, especially in his undying love for Catherine. He is a true romantic hero.

Ralph Fiennes and Juliette Binoche in *Wuthering Heights*, 1992

Mr Huntingdon and Branwell Brontë

Anne Brontë drew on her experience of her brother in her description of the drunken Huntingdon in *The Tenant of Wildfell Hall*. Helen Huntingdon describes him in her letter to Frederick:

'The invalid replied by groaning aloud, and rolling his head on a pillow in a paroxysm of impatience,

"I am in Hell, already!" cried he. "This cursed thirst is burning my heart to ashes! Will nobody—"

At the end of the novel Huntingdon is dead. *The Tenant of Wildfell Hall* was published in July of 1848; in September Branwell Brontë, too, had died.

Lord Byron (1788 - 1824)

Lord Byron was one of the great English Romantic poets. His work was well known to the Brontës and influenced their writing.

Lord Byron playing the part of a Romantic hero

The 'romantic' writers of the early nineteenth century all shared an interest in the supernatural, and in ideas about freedom of expression and the importance of the individual and his or her emotional life.

The romantic hero, such as Byron's characters Don Juan and Childe Harold, was an important element in the writing of the romantics. Such heroes were free thinkers, often rejected by society, driven by powerful emotions. These ideas were a starting point for characters such as Rochester and Heathcliff.

Powerful heroines

Autobiography in the novels

Many readers and critics today claim that the novels by the Brontës are based on their own lives, and the books are in some ways secret autobiographies. This is by no means the whole story.

Anne, Charlotte and Emily certainly used people, places and events in their lives in their novels. It is important to remember, though, two other vital ingredients – imagination, and the ability to tell stories. These skills were developed over the years as they devised their imaginary kingdoms of Glasstown and Gondal (see page 12), and in those evenings at the Parsonage where stories were told by the light of the flickering fire.

Catherine Earnshaw

Catherine, in *Wuthering Heights*, is a powerful and independent character, but not always an attractive one. She loves Heathcliff, and yet she marries Edgar 'because he will be rich, and I shall like to be the greatest woman of the neighbourhood.' Yet there is much more to Catherine than a spoilt, scheming woman. She is a contradictory character, a strange mixture of strength and weaknesses. She is able to love Edgar and Heathcliff at the same time, because her love for them is very different. Edgar is an earthly love, her love for Heathcliff a spiritual one. Yet despite her love for others, she is totally selfish and self-obsessed.

Juliette Binoche as Catherine (1992)

> 66 *Well, if I cannot keep Heathcliff for my friend – if Edgar will be a man and jealous – I'll try to break their hearts by breaking my own. That will be a prompt way of finishing all when I am pushed to extremity!* 99

In the end she betrays both men with the most selfish act of all – she brings about her own death. Emily Brontë was not at all like Catherine, but she too was a complex character. One side of her nature was deep and thoughtful. She was also a highly practical woman, effectively running the household at the Parsonage. Mrs Gaskell describes Emily busily making bread, 'which was always light and excellent', with a book propped up on the kitchen table.

Becky Sharpe – an anti-heroine

Vanity Fair by W M Thackeray was published at the same time as *Wuthering Heights*, but the novels are very different. If *Wuthering Heights* is set in the world of the imagination, *Vanity Fair* is very much the real world. The novel tells the life story of two heroines – Amelia, a trusting, unworldly character, and Becky Sharpe, a clever social climber. Becky is an orphan like Jane Eyre: she too becomes a governess. She secretly marries the eldest son of the family. Many adventures follow, with the deceitful, scheming Becky triumphing in the end.

Vanity Fair is a powerful satire on the materialistic society of the time.

Jane Eyre

Like her sister, Charlotte Brontë used one of her characters, in this case Jane Eyre, to express some of her own ideas. These were, though, much more worldly. Charlotte was interested in the issues of her time. Through Jane she challenged the view that one class was by nature better than another, and showed that the social order of the time was unjust and unfair, particularly to poor but well-educated women. In some ways, Jane Eyre is Charlotte's ideal woman, fiercely independent, and able to look the world in the eye without flinching. When Rochester describes Jane as an angel, she tells him:

> 66 *I am not an angel... and will not be one until I die; I will be myself. Mr Rochester, you must neither expect nor exact anything celestial of me – for you will not get it, any more than I shall get it of you; which I do not anticipate.* 99

A cover design for the 1847 edition of *Vanity Fair*

Brontë on Austen

Charlotte's Brontë's work was compared at the time with that of Jane Austen, but Charlotte was scathing of Austen's characters and style. This is what she wrote about *Pride and Prejudice*:

I would hardly like to live with her ladies and gentlemen in their elegant but confined houses.

Realism and imagination

Waiting for the reviews

Just as today, authors, especially those who had not published a book before, waited nervously for the reviews to appear in newspapers and magazines. Good reviews could mean a literary and financial success.

Generally, reviews for *Jane Eyre* were favourable, and the book was successful from the start. Charlotte Brontë would have been delighted to read the review that said 'we can cordially recommend *Jane Eyre* to our readers, as a novel to be placed at the top of the list to be borrowed, and to the circulating library keeper, as one which he may safely order. It is sure to be in demand.'

Some reviewers, however, thought that it was all a good deal too 'realistic' in the way it described its characters. 'The authors of *Jane Eyre*...' said one reviewer, 'have made the capital mistake of supposing that an artistic representation of character and manners is a literal imitation of individual life. The consequence is, that in dealing with vicious personages they confound vulgarity with truth, and awaken too often a feeling of unmitigated disgust.'

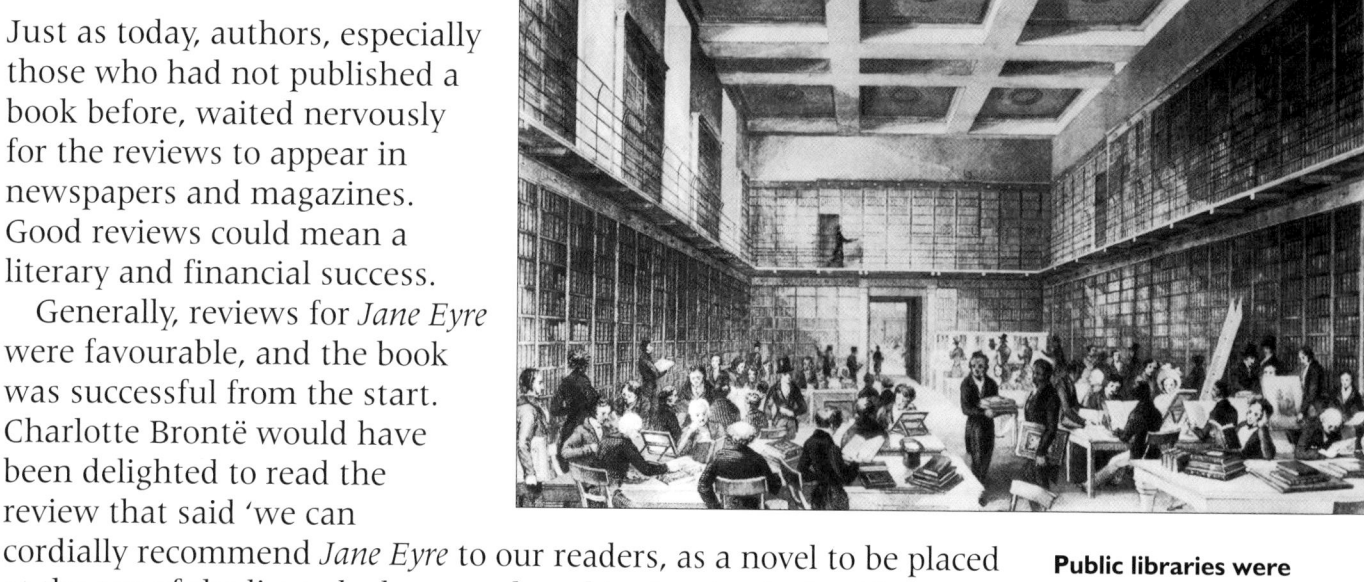

Public libraries were unusual at this time but the Reading Room at the British Museum was a popular haunt for literary figures in London.

'An offence against both politeness and good morals'

> **❝** *I've been greatly interested in Wuthering Heights, the first novel I've read for an age and the best (as regards power and sound style) for two ages... But it is a fiend of a book – an incredible monster... the action is laid in Hell, – only it seems places and people have English names there...* **❞**
>
> Dante Gabriel Rossetti, artist and poet

The reviews of *Wuthering Heights* were mixed. Many reviewers thought that there was far too much violence and horror. Some were shocked that expletives such as *Damn!* were written out in full; the usual practice was to use only the first letter: D— ! There was a

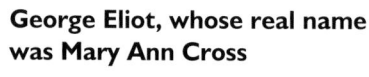

Yorkshire dialect

'And so ye've been murtherin' on him?' exclaimed Joseph, lifting his hands and eyes in horror. 'If iver I seed a seeght loike this!'
    Wuthering Heights, Chapter 17

Some of the early readers of the Brontës were baffled by the use of Yorkshire dialect in the books. The Brontës would have heard this from the local people, and especially from 'Tabby', Tabitha Aykroyd, their much-loved Yorkshire servant. The Brontës did not speak a Yorkshire dialect themselves. Writers at the time say they had Irish accents, which they acquired from their father.

feeling that literature shouldn't be about real life at all. '…it is the province of an artist to modify and in some cases refine what he beholds in the ordinary world,' said another reviewer. *Wuthering Heights*, even more than *Jane Eyre* before it, described people as they really were.

Even those critics who were strongly against the book recognised its power. The same reviewer who thought the book was 'an offence against politeness and good morals' admitted that it was 'original, powerful, and full of suggestiveness.' Like many readers, the critics may have hated the book – but they couldn't put it down!

66 *To represent a bad thing in its least offensive light is, doubtless, the most agreeable course for a writer of fiction to pursue; but is it the most honest, or safest?* 99
    Anne Brontë: introduction to the second edition of
    The Tenant of Wildfell Hall

Other writers

The comments that writers most like to hear are those of other authors. The great novelist and historian Thackeray wished he hadn't been sent a copy of *Jane Eyre*; he was very busy with his own work, but he couldn't stop reading it! He claimed that some of the love passages made him cry, to the astonishment of his servant when he came in to make up the fire. George Eliot was less enthusiastic; she thought the dialogue was written in a rigid, over-formal manner, more like police reports than a novel.

George Eliot, whose real name was Mary Ann Cross

The Brontës then and now

Elizabeth Gaskell (1810 - 1865) was a close friend of Charlotte. Following Charlotte's death, Mrs Gaskell wrote *The Life of Charlotte Brontë* at the request of Patrick Brontë.

Juliette Binoche in the 1992 version of *Wuthering Heights*

The life of Charlotte Brontë

Even though many critics were alarmed by the violence and 'coarseness' in the novels of the Brontë sisters, there was immediate recognition that they were enormously talented writers who had produced books of power and originality. Such was the interest in the Brontës, when their real identities were finally revealed, that Patrick Brontë asked Mrs Gaskell, the novelist and friend of Charlotte, to write an 'official' biography of his daughter – *The Life of Charlotte Brontë*.

This book was controversial from the beginning. In particular the author created a picture of Charlotte that was only part of the whole story. Her picture of a melancholy woman living a life of solitary suffering was not sufficiently balanced by mentioning her wit, sense of humour, and practical common sense. In *The Life of Charlotte Brontë* a legend was born. Like many legends, it is based on myth as well as the truth.

> 66 *It is well that the thoughtless critics, who spoke of the sad and gloomy views of life presented by the Brontës in their tales, should know how such work was wrung out of them by the living recollection of the long agony they suffered.* 99
>
> Elizabeth Gaskell, *The Life of Charlotte Brontë*

Modern views of the Brontë novels

The Brontë novels are as popular today as they have ever been. Emily is generally regarded as the greatest of the three. The themes of love and death, goodness and evil in *Wuthering Heights* will always fascinate readers. In recent years the novels of Charlotte and Anne have been seen as important in the development of the feminist movement, which has led to increasing popularity and critical study of

Jane Eyre and *The Tenant of Wildfell Hall*. The weaknesses in the novels – the over-wordy dialogue, the disjointed and over dramatic plots – are recognised today just as they were by the early reviewers. What is recognised now, far more than then, is the honesty of the novels. They attempted to portray people as they really were, without the gloss of conventionality and good taste expected of novels of the period.

'Brontëmania'

Haworth is still a difficult place to reach, although it can no longer be described as 'off the beaten track' – the track to Haworth has been well and truly beaten! It is second only to Shakespeare's Stratford in popularity as a literary site. These visits started soon after the publication of *The Life of Charlotte Brontë*. Even then local shopkeepers were cashing in by selling photographs of Patrick Brontë. Today this has turned into an industry. Some visitors see this as unpleasant commercialism and the Brontës would hardly recognise Haworth today. Even so, for the true Brontë enthusiast a visit to the Parsonage, with its museum, and to the unchanged landscape of the moors, will help them to understand the background to the genius of an extraordinary family.

'Script writing at the Brontës' by E H Shepard; a twentieth-century cartoonists' view of the Brontë household

Historical events		The life of the Brontës
American War of Independence	1775-83	
	1777	Patrick Brontë born
Peninsular War	1808-14	
Luddite riots	1811-15	
	1812	Patrick marries Maria Branwell
	1814	Maria Brontë is born
Battle of Waterloo	1815	Elizabeth Brontë born
	1816	Charlotte Brontë born, 21 April
	1817	Patrick Branwell Brontë born, 26 June
	1818	Emily Brontë born, 30 July
Peterloo riots; Keats writes *Ode to a Nightingale*	1819	
George IV comes to the throne. Walter Scott writes *Ivanhoe*	1820	Anne Brontë born, 17 January. Brontës move to Haworth
Death of Napoleon	1821	Mrs Brontë dies
First passenger railway, Stockton-Darlington	1825	Two elder girls, Maria and Elizabeth, die
	1826	Remaining Brontë children begin writing stories
Death of George IV: William IV comes to throne	1830	
	1831-32	Charlotte at Roe Head school
Great Reform act. Middle classes get the vote	1832	
Abolition of slavery in the British Empire	1833	
	1835	Emily at Roe Head school
Death of William IV: Queen Victoria comes to the throne	1837	
Dickens writes *Oliver Twist*	1838	Emily becomes a governess
Beginning of the Chartist movement	1839	Anne and Charlotte become governesses
Introduction of penny post	1840	
	1842	Charlotte and Emily study at a school in Brussels
Beginning of potato famine in Ireland	1845	

HISTORICAL EVENTS		THE LIFE OF THE BRONTËS
Abolition of the Corn Laws	**1846**	Poems by the Brontë sisters published under pseudonyms
	1847	*Jane Eyre* by Charlotte Brontë published in October. *Wuthering Heights* (Emily Brontë) and *Agnes Grey* (Anne Brontë) published in December
Karl Marx writes *The Communist Manifesto*	**1848**	*The Tenant of Wildfell Hall* (Anne Brontë) published. Branwell dies, 24 September. Emily dies, 19 December
	1849	Anne dies, 28 May *Shirley* (Charlotte Brontë) published
The Great Exhibition	**1851**	
	1853	*Villette* (Charlotte Brontë) published
Beginning of the Crimean War	**1854**	Charlotte marries the Rev. A. B. Nicholls
	1855	Charlotte dies, 31 March
Charles Darwin publishes *The Origin of Species*	**1859**	
	1861	Patrick Brontë dies, 7 June.

Index

Further reading

The Brontë novels are available in a number of paperback editions, some very inexpensive. The Penguin English Library editions have excellent introductions. Useful study guides are available in the York notes series and the Macmillan Master Guides.

Selected poems by the Brontës is published by J M Dent.

Two excellent general books on the Brontës have the same title; *The Brontes*. The book by Juliet Barker (published by Weidenfeld and Nicholson) is a substantial modern account of their life and work. The book by Phyllis Bentley (Thames and Hudson) covers the life of the Brontes and is very well illustrated. Other important books are the biographies by Winifred Gerin, *Emily Brontë and Anne Brontë*, and *The Life of Charlotte Brontë* by Elizabeth Gaskell.

Internet:

A description of 'Brontë country' can be visited at http://www.yorkshire.co.uk.brontecountry. The Brontë Parsonage Museum Website ia at bronte.org.co.uk. There is also a Web-site for students of the Brontës at http://www.hevelius.demon.co.uk/bronte/

There are many other Web-sites devoted to the Brontës and their work.

Places to visit

The Brontë Society
The society is based at The Brontë Parsonage Museum, Haworth, Keighley, West Yorkshire BD22 8DR. There are concessionary rates for students.

The Museum
The Brontë Parsonage Museum (address above) is open all the year round except at Christmas and for four weeks from mid January. Phone 01535 642323